The Land of Give and Take

TYLER FARRELL

salmonpoetry

Published in 2012 by
Salmon Poetry
Cliffs of Moher, County Clare, Ireland
Website: www.salmonpoetry.com
Email: info@salmonpoetry.com

Copyright © Tyler Farrell, 2012

ISBN 978-1-907056-95-6

COVER ARTWORK: *Untitled, mixed media on paper by Kyle Fitzpatrick – kylefitzpatrick.com*
COVER DESIGN: *Siobhán Hutson*

For my wife, Joan and our two sons, Holden and Linus.
For poets: James Liddy *(in memory)*, Jim Chapson,
Eamonn Wall and Cynthia Belmont.

My thanks, also, to fellow Salmon poet and friend,
Emily Wall, who read and commented on some
of these poems in their infancy.

And yet and yet
Is this my dream, or the truth?

W. B. YEATS

He kept young as one who tells the truth keeps young.

JAMES LIDDY

Acknowledgements

Thanks are due to the editors of the following in which some of these poems have previously appeared:

Burdock, REAL: Regarding Arts and Letters, The Solitary Plover, Yemassee, Free Lunch, Paddlefish, ELM: Eureka Literary Magazine, Art and Ethos of Dubuque, The Recorder, Cooweescoowee, Fire Ring Voices, Gallery / Writer's Guild, and *The Blue Canary.*

Contents

I. The Honest to God Truth

II. Journals to _____

III. The Exaggeration of Everything

I. The Honest to God Truth

Even if a thing is true it by no means follows that one is bound to reveal it.

LORD ALFRED DOUGLAS
Oscar Wilde: A Summing Up

And not satirically or humorously true, but simply the truth. Pure unadulterated truth—luminous, profound and essential.

SIMONE WEIL
in a last letter to her parents

A Found Postcard

Dear Alyce-
Just a card to let you know
we got the "letter" you
sent to Jerry at Camp Carson –
Cashed it already.
Going uptown soon.
Arrived yesterday in the middle
of a parade honoring
the founder of Denver.
Have driven farther
now than ever before.
Still all the news I know.
Thanks again. Love and Kisses.
                    –Bernice

The Influence of Joyce and Clarke on the Loss of My Faith

Politics in the summer sermons of my youth
like fiends thrown overboard at the first
instance of lust and love and sex with slight
girlfriends. The hell of voices sighing,
waiting for repentance while the priest
reaches inside his pocket to adjust his
microphone. The way the old ladies fawn
over him like a flock of sheep, moocows
lowing at the classics, the bible studies
on Sunday and the choir directed by Sister
Bernadette who broke her arm at the news
of runaways, shocked, smoking pot under
the slide at Wilson park. The breath of God,
the anger casting lawgivers like a voice
of conscience. I remember dispensation
by the Pope on St. Patrick's Day and talk
of celibacy and gluttony, the shadowed
miles of the mind, the temptation when
Junior High was more stress than college,
like suffering sinners crying at the feet
of Lucifer. I stood at the base of the statue
of Mary and watched her crush the serpent
with her bare feet. The sisters talked of
doubt, proper handwriting, hovering
above us like dark angels filled with eyes
and sight for the low classes of people
too poor to give to the church. Saint
Catherine of Siena would rather walk
a track of red coals than gaze upon the face
of the devil again. She prayed a solemn hush,
instead of luscious fields in the morning
mist where sloth and pride ran in the dark
flashing torches like candles at the head

of a deathbed. The modern church was
lines around our eyes, fell from the ceiling
every Wednesday and a sample of shrines
beheld in the form of grottoes, sand in my
hands. The small souls sign their names on
pages and pages of dollar bills in order
to witness the shaking of hands, thrown
dirt over shoulders and into the graveyard.
The new church renovated with fear
and low words. They taught me to wonder
at the start of our hours, the flesh of the
Crucifix and not of humans where blood
dripped on the heads of the damned.
The heavens were a roar, children of
some soul cleansed by baptism. The fires
rekindle with a birth in flame and I sit
with my mind in a book. The essence
and glow somehow stained my eyes,
but the sight has opened a way in void
of spirit, the walls of clay, the shapeless
body, the word, the language of myself.
The bleak rain and phantoms have gone
and the refuge of sinners has been cured
by Saint Thomas, the angelic doctor,
the divine light where spirits of the un-
defiled Virgin rekindling my thoughts
on a plain bench reading of youth, age,
sinners, saints, mortals torn from a book
by my Gods. All worship and revere
the truest of all sins, the Bible without
judgment, the counsel of highest nature,
the holy words of your two Irish sons.

The Truth of Angels and Ravens

If you have ever read an autobiography
of an Angel you know
they first kiss every page, then let
them float bound with white hair
in the morning mist of sunshine
until they drop
into the mailbox of God.
If God rejects the submission
(for he gets far more
than he can possibly publish)
he summons a raven
to collect the words – the small
symbols for mankind to decipher – and ties
them to a black feathered back
with golden string made from
stolen ingots confiscated from wall street
embezzlers and big business
brokers. Then the raven swoops down
to earth and drops the manuscript
at a bus stop, or train depot,
or alley way in Brooklyn to watch
the words blow like wind waves
of everyday lives.
And that is how we know
Angels write quite exaggerated
prose about the possibility of their existence.

Ode to Father Jacques Marquette and Louis Joliet (May Day 1673)

Louis,
what philosopher
are you reading tonight
under upper Midwest stars?
Perhaps Plato
or Aristotle?
I am partial to poetry
by Crashaw.
He is one of the converted.
Read him in the pine forest
with a pipe after mass
while the shadows
of fur bearing
mammals expire.
The beaver pelt
for Jacques' birthday
will provide warmth
to kindle this, his sacrifice.

And you, Fr. Marquette,
with Jesuit wonders
of making
the Portage (Wisconsin)
and eventual descent down
the west bank
of the Mississippi
only to miss your
chance at becoming
the very first
New Orleans sinner.
Instead,
you ascend
once again

and join the savages
near the river
before nightfall
to say mass.

St. Ignace pray for our sins.

Mid-Afternoon at a Barn outside Platteville

The narrow garden
still in light
where suns shine over
ricks of hay.
A red barn protects
those shorn
in a corner to fit.
Under clouds as
vision snows sing
like the first
coat of frost.
The dark grates
smell of heather.
Dance the water fields.
A mere slip
under ice
and light boycotts
the earth in fall.
There tumbles
relief, the flailing
fields learning
to lust.
This private delight
fills my eyes,
dips my face
into a sound stream.

Three Poems for James Liddy

The Apartment of James Liddy

Those gossip eyes waking when I arrive
and senses gained in the small light
of the sitting room while Jim gets us
tea and puts down his copy of Pepys'
Diary in order to talk and recite, tales
of teachers and poetry in dark winter
nights when the hallway red staircase
glows with whispers from Milwaukee.
James joins us and immediately asks
for the news of old friends, students
now around the globe, books of thoughts
from those who don't always confide
in him, but probably should. Liddy
is a champion of youth, a champion
of words from youth, an announcement
still ringing in the ears of a Blue Canary
sent down from heaven to gather holy
words from this Irish and American
wide eyed author, this Papal edict
given us forever in these times of need.
Then Jim goes to his room to pray and read,
a monastic life amidst a city backdrop
and James checks the knobs on the stove
to make sure they have been turned off.
We enter the street, hope for adventure
to see a slow moving world where bars
seem the only savior and poetry has been
taught as a life, filtered through this man,
this friend whom I admire for his memory,
his knowledge and stories. Luckily, like
for Hartnett, he has agreed to be the one to
teach me to be a poet in the coming days.

At the Bookshop

I have wandered through the dirtiest of bookshops
searching for yet another talented, unknown author
I can mention to my friends. But most don't seem
to care about writers or even that I worked in a few
bookshops, but was fired due mostly to reading
books instead or shelving or re-arranging or general
work a tome laborer should be doing during work hours.
Hell! They could pay me and I'd smell the books,
sleep in piles of books, have engorged dreams about
stacks of books whispering to me as I sip a beer
in a red velvet chair and recite from secondhand copies
of paperback Irish literature anthologies crying of
distant heavens and hells, religion from the Roman
Empire, miracle fresh water words flow to the river.
Heroes & wisdom count toward eternal salvation
and happiness. Much like a lover whispering a truth
in your ear under peaceful skies. She says, "I love you,
I love you" again (never often enough) "I love you."

Saints in Madrid, Iberian Sons

We thought light had blinded the tourists.
No one at the Prado except school children,
loud and abundant school children
with open mouths, backpacks, plotting eyes.
I saw you at the foot of the steps
with your fingers in your ears looking
toward the knick-knack carts full of pictures
of Spanish Saints. St. Teresa, her habit.
God strolls here to buy Gaudí trinkets,
yard bells, postcards, bull shirts & pottery.
Art like vespers, words like evening mass
when the sun curled round the earth.
I bought a bullfighter's jacket, red with
jangly, golden fringe, acted out the killing
of a bull in front of you. You squinted,
told me of Hemingway. In older days,
meat from gored horses went to the poor.
More armor and the peasants now starve.
At the bar, cervesas frio. Praise Spain!
The inspired age, Hartnett in residence,
Isabella's Prayer book, silent private chapel.
The bartender saw us praying together,
asked, "Mas Cervesas?" You replied,
"Si, of course." Drinks arrived, you intoned,
"Protect us, Saint Mary of the Winds,
Winged Mother of Isabella's Spain,
Protector and Queen of the Catholic world."
We bowed our heads, then took the cup.

Three Poems for Joyce and Beckett

Thoughts for James Joyce on Bloomsday, 2009

The heart is a son
made from a world of whispered names.
He makes us beg for secrets
in dark forests.
Trees peak still like Ireland
lit by a century of new slogans.
We are clothed in ancient flesh
borrowed like God's candles
burnt down for cracks in wooden faces.
We make out lilies by the sea
faint white avenues in air
pavements where canes step down
coat sleeves beat a gesture from light.

Easter with Samuel Beckett (Born on Good Friday)

Upstairs my wife's family is having house church.
Pause (louder)
Downstairs I'm waiting for Godot.

Poem Written on James Joyce's Birthday, Feb 2, 2010

Clear glass eye-patch,
Mass card labyrinth.
I can see your sugar of roses
marchpane
foul pleasures in the spring
emblazoned on a bench
inside Dublin,
pipe smell of burn.
A long letter
costs half a crown,
parchment caresses the skin.
Tremble now, say yes.

Up to the Minute News Reporting

Here lives a certain time
a fading light
something that unravels in the afternoon.
Here we render notices
for the families,
steel trains loading media,
spouting logos like
God is dead
lower your Cholesterol
consume more anti-oxidants
reach for job security
in untimely hours
of a fluctuating economy.
Souls starve a desperate need
for reinvention,
like children on gravel roads
throwing time
into barren and blonde fields,
constructing excuses for an education.
One in four teenage girls claim an STD,
one in three teenage boys forgets why
he got involved in the first place.
But we are all young
with our struggling minds,
our issues, our homes of failed marriages,
our tremendous guilt
our unabashed pride.
We are two sides,
two faces, two lives in a world
leaving chilled churches
for heated streets.

The True Nature of Catholicism

Where could, or maybe when could
nature ever rival religion?
Give it a run for its money
in rain slickers
with waves pounding the surf
and tsunamis of biblical proportion.

Some see a connection:
Pope John Paul II, the lake poets.
Also, theologians and mystics who talked
of the indifference of God,
infinite contradictions and endless relevance.

But all of us must look at truth
through the mystery and ministry of life.
The wilderness stretched out in front of our eyes.
A place of divine love given down this barren earth.

Therefore, why make certain rules?
Laws with Papal edicts to stop chaos in the universe.
This Proclamation, for example:
No wedding ceremonies outside.

Why? For lack of mosquitoes?
For the sanctity of the house of Peter's rock?
Perhaps.
However, I believe the Church
might not want the unpredictability.
But mainly, it couldn't handle the miraculous competition.

Pray for all that is clear and bright,
more that is beautiful and abundant.

Jane Gallop's Phone Monkey

Footsteps in the hall,
lumber with love apples
sheltered in leopard skin
hair dye, mountain fear,
intimidation, island dawn.
Door creaks down Curtin hall
fourth floor, grey and beige
in the white light of office hours,
genius student requests,
pleadings for direction, ass kissing
lip kissing, heavy petting.
My phone is her phone.
It rings like newlyweds
always at this hour, this minute.
Rings in English, German,
Postmodern Poetry translated
the way only professors could.
My body though a silver
frame like heaven opening
a gate, St. Peter and his big book
allowing me entrance.
"It's for you," I say.
"For me?" she says in surprise.
Like she didn't know
or at least suspect.
Then I turn and hear her
cackle on the receiver
and walk down to my
un-famous cube, feel
her eyes on my backside
loving my every step,
every one hour week.
My unlikely turn
as her little grad boy,
her quiet office assistant.

Mass in Rice Lake, Wisconsin

My mother-in-law
knows all the angles
when it comes to
negotiating Saturday night
mass schedules and times.
Even without running water
she still looks pure
and virginal readying
herself to pray
for all the sinners
in her life, including myself.
Her husband always
says she hasn't met
a kneeler she didn't like.
And the kids pile out
of the car. I grab
my book and head
for the Saturday pizza
place while the rest sit
through a long Mass
filled with songs and words,
the old people standing,
then sitting in trance.
Ladies in white robes, voices
from the choir loft
as the priest clears
his throat and adjusts
his microphone. Before
I leave she says to me,
"I think we'll get out
in an hour. But you never know
with confirmation season."
So I sit in the pizza place,
drinking a beer, reading

my book while waiting
for someone to complain
that I have twelve seats
saved for the Catholics
on their way for reward.
Lord only knows when
they will arrive.

Looking for the Ghost of Fr. Roseliep

Your catholic eyes for sacrifice
covered in vocation,
serving small rain
on the streets of Dubuque.

This trinity of devotion
for teaching, poetry, and sanctity
like a gold leaf path,
a human form in elegy.

I thought I saw you staring
down from the seminary walls,
watching footsteps
on the fallen rocks carved
in the years of stolen bluffs.

Where did you pour
those "waterpots of gin?"
Those half-truths of bedfellows
and dark hair flaming
in the gaslight of your room.

The small prick from a shadow,
morning bells ringing
in the sun and last year's
silence like a dream.

You climbed that hill
in June with a patch work quilt
and hyphens blown
through the willows.
The credo and tyranny of God
in the sunken hills
of a river town.

On Hearing that an Old Hotel in Downtown Dubuque is Scheduled for Demolition

Those red bricks mix
with clouds
in a bluff wind
of yesterday
no longer knocking
on the window of light.

What young men will
grieve for her
upstream on the dirty river
while doorways
into evening whiten.
Children play in her
shadow, sweetness drowned
by boys who walk
with their lips
and listen
with their mouths.

Protesters pack lunches
put on winter clothes
chain themselves to trees
plead with politicians
who act like statues
in the sun.
Most walk by
with heads down
filled with boredom
on their way
to a casino to throw
money at sorrows.

Monday daybreak brings
bulldozers.
Some search
for lists of city fathers.
I think they are kept
by the blind
man at the bookstore.
You must read
the price to him.
He lets you get
your own change.

Five Short Poems

A Quick One for John Berryman

O Henry
with threats
of jumping
out of windows.
What shape
is your
beard now?
Perhaps round,
like a song.

Manuscripts for the Digital Age

I finished scanning Liddy's poems
for the Selected
and e-mailed them to John Redmond.

Then I sat down and wrote this poem.
Scanned it as well.

Work

When loss of your jump drive
strikes panic in your heart.

Woodland Pattern Poet

O Antler,
where has your beard gone?
Burned by a campfire
or stolen
by forest fairies
and woven
into God's hairshirt?
Then worn on the head
of a Northland College graduate.

Ode to Drinking a Schlitz amidst Protests

Joe McCarthy and Scott Walker.
The politicians who made Milwaukee famous.

The Fleeting Avenues of Summer

The avenues of summer
will not last
and cabstands will seem
further from bars,
a windbreaker under one arm.
The golden age of memoir
is on these streets.
These glared windows
and pavement reflections,
where glad hands
throw cigarettes down
at each crack in the sidewalk,
a front stoop painted green,
an outdoor beer garten,
a yellow brick building.
A breath of lake water air
through windows
flung open in houses of charm,
on pedestrian streets,
in grids of near city blocks.

The Burning Shadow

for Kate O'Brien

Saint Teresa of Ávila
soul servant and truth author
love's full quiver of life and death
play long with that breath.

What bright soul,
flaming heart in Castilian girls
wise like the spirit flower
of the civilized world.

In scarce dawn, rebirth
convinces lucky children
to profess life everlasting –
vision of power, immediate.

Hymn to a Martyr

for Richard Crashaw

> *But our having parents seemed to us a very great hindrance.*
> ST. TERESA OF ÁVILA, *The Book of Her Life*

Let us out grow our parents
together, and go now,
you and I,
to the land of the Moors
and be beheaded there
so we may live
as martyrs,
blood enough
for salvation.
The heart's cabinet suffers.
Open the purple wardrobe
of your side
to love a divine
and sacred flame.
Imitate saints, unto thee.
Desire eternity.
Forever and ever,
Amen.

The Lord Giveth

(Poem for Michael Hartnett)

Crucifix classrooms, twelve of age
I learned of joyful verse hymns too.
Old fathers like a whiskey sage,
rain words, drenched in comment dew.

Preach on truthful pen,
from Liddy's mouth as well.
Your stolen cat or necklace wren.
Arena, what immaculate spell.

Abandoned language, cliché love
which bore my chalice, cursed the air.
Pubs near the Liffey, Kavanagh above.
Yellowed pictures and witness here.

The night now surrounds us most,
your face in flame emblazoned.
A risen star from such a host
with words and thought so wizened.

Consider this one holy truth.
Limerick, south Newcastle West.
A son gathers surrounded with
unbound truthful quips as quest.

Poem for Lorine Niedecker

As I paint the streets
I melt the houses

Your face is the weather
your eyes the rain–

forever cultivates
my thoughts
on what stands
for beauty these days.

Stand by the boatman
and know
his rough face sways

away
        from your chin.
        Variance

without and within.

God's Chosen People

The northern earth of fragrant birth, 1835.
Mock the envious eye, confound the reckoning.
A tale of hinterland clergy.
Daily conversions of Ojibway souls,
once alone on Bayfield peninsula.

Save the savage face.
Shepard their souls
with meekness and love,
and nature's white hand.

Fr. Frederic Baraga, the snowshoe priest,
had a tongue for languages
and Adam's brow.
One mind to make it understood
how God considers any man and his fall.

Missions at Cross river.
Church and cemetery
now shrine to safe landings and crystal flesh.
Life everlasting for the unclaimed.
Thread of flesh alive in time's race.

He promoted health care and small pox vaccinations.
Denounced liquor in demijohns: the curse of the tribe.

He even learned the native language.
Printed a book, the first any soul had seen.
Then came more: Catechism, prayer guides,
bible stories spoken by the tongue of the land.

Father knew the power of the word.
The importance of language. The arrow of light.
A seraphim soul instructor
who speaks the body's birth language,
tells of an origin without sin.

Poem in Honor of Austin Clarke's Reverence

Great and spiritual woes, that odium theologicum
which overshadows our childhood.
There was always a tiny ringing in the ear;
a soul in purgatory crying to us for aid.

I imagined my Jesuit self-aware education
(beneath the cloud of unknowing) to be similar.
The times would keep me from seeing the black church
or tempt the fates by running twice round it.

I admired how you saw the secret pool,
discovered another hemisphere in which all was different.
Walked among golden crosses on lapels of priests and brothers
melting in the round glow of gas rings.
Would you dare scribble light thoughts of repression,
sadistic celibacy, sensual interests on the Magnificat?

I often pray to you St. Austin, venerate you,
for your blessings obtained from God,
to dispel our fears in reverential radiance, lovely and enskied.
Thank you for illuminated words on dark volumes.
Knowledge of the hypnotizing gaze, the tortured darkness of apostasy.

Like the martyr St. Denis after being decapitated.
He picked up his head and walked a mile.

A Topic for the Confessional

At the Galway Bus Station
two blown kerchiefs speak
above rain dotted black dresses
from the nuns in disguise. Humid
students wait for lines to subside.
Coffee, a mist in the afternoon.
Schedules on tables slip down
like dark hair over a small girl's eyes.
The music from the street
drops in the air and the book
I have just read invigorates me
like the rain has baptized me.
The bus will still not be here
for a little while. But I clutch
my sparkling water and wonder
if I should ask those nice
nuns if they want to go get
a drink with me in the pub
across the street. But I am not
going to tell you if I actually did
ask those kind nuns to have a
pint with me. That's between
me, them, and God now.

Writing Grants for Notebooks

Important assistants in offices
often practice their hands
at requesting grant money
for everything a grade and middle school needs.
New basketball uniforms,
polished gym floors shined once a year.
Blue tile for the atrium, recent addition.
Formica tables in the rec room.
Large maps of an ever changing world.
New books for the library.
Teaching aids for 21st century students.
Curriculum wants what curriculum gets.
But still, the aged Pastor wonders
why they want so much money to buy notebooks.
A woman just back from lunch says,
"They're not the spiral kind of notebooks, Father."

The Renovation of the Shelbourne Hotel

Stone guard gutted,
covered in golden sheets
of Bowen.
She haunts the rooms,
hits on her chambermaids.

Elizabeth, how big was your house?

As big as a hotel
packed with carriage streets
and children for land
near St. Stephen's Green.

The butcher and newsagent
each lit a smoke while
blue shed a bedroom sanctuary.

Perhaps Liddy is in the horseshoe lounge
telling of youthful Dublin
with Mother and her heavenly
Clare accent.

Lent

*I wish ye a merry Lent; I hate Lent, I hate different diets,
and Furmity & Butter, & herb Porridge, and sour devout
faces of People who only put on Religion for 7 weeks.*

JONATHAN SWIFT, *Journal to Stella*

Will I be sent to everlasting damnation
in Dante's levels of Hell
if I enjoy Lent simply for a Friday fish fry?

I love to see those long lines of Catholics
winding around a neighborhood chapel
in wondrous blue spring light
so they may sit in a church basement
to be seen by white collared priests,
families with wide eyed children,
important parishioners stuffing their faces.

I see some pious old ladies talking of others,
devoting themselves to giving up sweets
for 40 days and nights, hands intertwined with powder
pink rosaries – the only sin, one of pride.

But perhaps they are saying a Hail Mary
for gluttonous bodies
as they watch me gorge myself
on the trough of the oldest established Christian faith.

St. Patrick and St. Catherine pray for our swollen souls.
Pray for Papal dispensation and for all believers
now and at the hour of our appetite, Amen.

Three Catholic Prayers

A Morning Prayer for Our Blessed Virgin Mary

The fridge sounds like a rainstorm
while I sit and read a new book, learn about
The Roman Catholic Chapel at Knock.
I can almost see the dry spot,
under a brown gable, then
the apparition of the Virgin Mary,
her Son
and St. John the Evangelist
on the cutting board altar
raised under Thy invocation
blessing our names in this small kitchen.
From rain to full day shine.
Now, perhaps I'll shanks' mare to mass
and hope the homily is brief.

Prayer for Pope Benedict XVI and His Love of Abstinence

Parts of deepest Africa
are gaining more Catholics
than the U.S. is losing.
They may hold us into
the next millennium
if we pray
for the new wave,
the next tide,
a cure for the epidemic
without the use of condoms.
Besides,
the rare book room
at the Vatican Library
needs more rubber gloves.

Prayer In Thanksgiving for Learning Chess from a Priest

Slow and deliberate.
Contemplate.
Of all the moves in heaven and earth
you must protect Mary,
Queen of Angels, mother of us all.

The Lives of the City, Long Forgotten

We have seen them
in the sky, in the trees,
among the fog
that rises from a winter earth
covered by snow
white on ice
like the Mississippi.

We have felt them
with our hands,
the sounds blamed on breath,
streets and houses
like steel pillars
next to a subway station,
shadows from darkened windows.

They are full, like pomegranates,
small seeds from the ground
that look like a heart
greeting a new child,
a small direction for a finger
to point out our flaws
nearly shown
from a wrinkled face.

We have told others of them,
their good work
and, like outstretched hands,
their lives naked
to amuse ourselves.

There is morning and night
to see through their eyes.
There are amusements
to be told, invented,

two historians that begin a game.
One may greet you
on the road to the city,
the other sits on a bridge
and waits to be asked
about his legacy,
that face with many
grains of distance.

Cameras One through Five

I can see only straight lines in all directions.
A bank teller on a break
followed by battered shapes
of structure. I look into windows and shards of glass
in full form waiting to break.
Peer with me, squint your eyes and focus
on what makes you watch. I am
drawn in thousands
of ways, images obscured by rain,
street lights and college girls telling stories
of last night's break up. Get closer,
get closer to you in every way
and answer my calls only when I need
to feel the hot fog on the back of my lens.
The skyline ropes another piece of sky
and nobody stops for a second to look up.
They worry about their wound up movements
like toys clambering their way through
crowded streets of afterthoughts
of what I should have done different last night.
Maybe another drink and she would have
taken me home. Maybe a talk with my girlfriend.
Maybe dealing with my boss. Maybe a slight
switch of judgment if I wasn't thinking
about his clothes on the floor of that hotel room.
Maybe a turn of a key in the front lock
of my parent's house. Maybe a trip to the south
side for a beer with my friends. Maybe a cab
ride instead of the bus. Maybe a dollar
to that man outside the Laundromat. Maybe
a shoe shine from the machine
in the bathroom. Maybe if you listened
you could hear what I see.

II.

A funeral procession long after
the trial of walking
on top of frozen sidewalks.
Who can see the streets the way I can?
The man on the corner always
waits for a bus, but never knows
that I am looking over his shoulder
and hollering at those business men
jaywalking in broad daylight
and security guards
asleep at their desks, a cup
of coffee slowly going cold.
The steam evaporates in another
25 seconds. Sigh again
and again without a touch of irony
like those altar boys after Sunday service
and the piazza with men on covered
streets and blacktop faces.
Tonight, I want to go dancing.
He says to himself, "Did I turn the iron off?"
while checking his watch
and rubbing a finger under his nose.
I can see what he is hiding
behind that worn face, but only his clients
will never know the deeds of insecure men.

III.

The bank is steady today, the swinging
door is always revolving. It spills
out red ties with a symmetrical geometry
by and by, a frame within a frame.
Consistent and formal, nobody
stops to ask directions
to a restaurant down the street.

The vault is impenetrable, but
I keep my left eye on it at all times.
Who is the man in the trench coat?
A simple sign of a check and the cash is yours,
no questions asked. A cynic would
demand more. The windows are darkened
with sight and I wonder what it would
be like to be free of the upper corner
of a white stucco ceiling. No matter.
The cell needs recharging, the monitors
are wearing thin. My lens needs
a good cleaning and an upgrade
is on its way from the factory.
A man in a white hat fiddled with my knobs
on Tuesday. Let me keep looking
into your eyes. I can focus automatically
on people with flesh exposed and trade
insults on attire and hair and wonder
where she is going tonight. But I know
it is back to an abusive husband. And he
is testing new torture devices in his basement.
And he doesn't live with his mother
anymore because she died a week ago
after a long struggle with cancer. And she hasn't
told her boyfriend that she is sleeping with
his roommate. And he has nothing to hide except
his shame. And she is someone with a terrible urge
to need. And he is stealing from his foreman
to support his habit. And she hasn't told her parents
about her boyfriend. And he is someone
without any happiness for the place that he
has been stuck inside since high school.
Like I said, I can focus automatically.

IV.

My kingdom to be a fly on the wall
and all I have is you, the Friday
afternoon crowd who are much
younger and move faster. A roll of
quarters here, and stack of bills there.
Teach me a new trick so I can
look inside. I can hear things too,
but can only comprehend images,
a filtering of lives in another
part of the city where being
is always another crime. I am obscure
to most, but a child looks and nods
his approval. No matter, the tapes
will be erased in a fortnight
and I will forget why I zoomed in.
What is she wearing today? Another
silk scarf from her lover. Another braided
anklet of iron sulfate to show
to her co-workers. Another bruise on her arm
and some quick cash for enough drinks.
I want to dance tonight with his
feet. I want to stretch out
among the living, but the lights
will be turned off at midnight
and my tape will go unused
in darkness. There is a bar just down
the street and I hear they are installing us
in the bathrooms and selling the tapes to
a network. My reward is filled with the innards
of hopeful and despicable people. I don't ask
for flesh, just to know such secrets.

V.

A public harangue out front,
I focus on its name
transcribed in human chatter
and sermonized with an influence
on the public. Music always covers up
what is being talked about while the cops
are in the wrong bar looking
for the wrong man. Public domain
is always used instead of common sense.
I hope that the security guard
is asleep again so I can see this alone.
One by one they all collapse outside
and only I have access to their inner thoughts,
their honest accusations about mothers
and fathers out in public. If one knows
he is being recorded, one always acts
as if a role had been chosen for him, a movie
camera and a director forming a box with
his thumbs and first fingers.
I want to be who I am showing you
not who I am ashamed to tell you.
A flirting persona, confident and humorous,
followed by nights of guilt and anger, of drinking
too much and late night television
when I should be reading or throwing
out boxes of past newspapers with articles
about who reviles me and when.
I am looking over his shoulder
and documenting what he sees
from inside the trench coat and briefcase
of an average man
trying to make it in this world.
The eyes of a saint are often traded
for one moment of sin.

II. Journals to _____

I'll tell you a sore truth, little understood.
JOHN MONTAGUE
"No Music"

Men are sometimes hanged for telling the truth.
ST. JOAN OF ARC
from her trial

I Have Spent My Life

to the memory of dear Liam O'Connor

> *…in the perpetual sign of loss and gain*
> JAMES LIDDY

I have spent my life on the hopes of people,
on the love intentions of the furious and silent.
Now, fallen away snapshots in the nightwar,
the war in the belly of its survivors, the ones
who have given up asking nothing more for the hardship.

I have felt like storms and like droughts,
heard words from Christ's politicians
who drink for the wrong reasons,
make grand statements about current fiscal crises,
offer food to a stolen child, disassembled.
Return them to the separate house world,
tell them to behave and accept.

I have been made to choose
between the rich and the ignorant,
petty thieves of the moral right and the ethic wrong.

I have spent money earned over years
before I knew what to spend it on.
I will keep earning and spending. Until it's all spent.
I will pass on knowledge to my sons, the heirs
to a world whose dead are set in their ways.
The living under similar ground and salvation.

The lies told by adults help them reach adulthood.
Something new like the unvarnished truth, gently and gradually.
They grow up a little every day.
Some play make-believe in overpriced houses
with little pets and buried in-laws in the root cellar,
a family bible strapped to their chest.
Make a world with endless torments of hell.

Let us pray.
>O master you are all knowing.
>You have given us the numbered lights in the sky.
>For which to count our blessings by.

I have been let in with light and woken to the sound of rails.
Love received and I value the gift highly.

I have covered my wounds to serve myself and my family.
If it were necessary to suffer more, I would.
But I am humble while the wind from city grates
rolls back to the great lake.

I have confessed to no one,
the feeling of sorrow and the fullness of pleasure.
Made charts for my school, my jobs, my mistakes.
I have drunk imaginary milk
from an imaginary glass.

A little boy crossed over Wisconsin Ave. today
with his pregnant mother and I started to cry out of joy.
I spent the rest of the day thinking
about possible occupations for those children.
Banker, Stunt Driver, Weaver, Rover.
The next obsolete occupation of the future.
Rejoice! Rejoice!

Let us pray.
>O master you are all knowing.
>You have given us the numbered lights in the sky.
>For which to count our blessings by.

I have awoken again.
I have spent the day in the city on the lookout
for clues for the laypeople,
instructions to the day and night,
confessions from the discretion closet.

I have spent my life in thought
dispensing an abundance of virtues and fullness,
intentions to pass along, always useful, perhaps misguided.
Made one place my home, another, my head.
The future believes in my current self.
The past forgets my older self.
I will think and love, truth seek and commend.
How have I spent my life?

Let us pray.
> O master you are all knowing.
> You have given us the numbered lights in the sky.
> For which to count our blessings by.

Going Through Withdrawal over Someone I Almost Fell in Love With

...and the prettiest girls in the world live in Des Moines.

JACK KEROUAC, *On the Road*

My cell phone has stopped ringing
ever since you left Dubuque
the day after I left Dubuque
asking me to stay with you
in that big empty house on a bluff
for just one more beer,
one deep conversation about you or me or us.
The way we always talked,
the varied topics we used to discuss
when we were drunk and felt young
and still in that life instead of this life
that happened after these descriptive days
you are now reading or hearing,
the words from the middle of our new lives.
However, I am speaking
of your new life in your capitol
and my current life in my capitol.
It is in this new life I wish your happiness,
in this new life I hope you are well.

I Wrestled With You in this Poem

for Jack Spicer

Her legs
could be California.
Her empty eyes,
rivers.

Mud bank
strangers
fishing
for bewildered birds.

I lived
a forest.
Sang with giant trees,
a sacred noise.

Her face
cannot sleep.
Up from the heart,
mirrored glen hunters.

Flame – ghost bird.
Claw – visible ocean.

Camera pointed
toward
the orbit.
Temporary, not flat, voices.

Spiritland,
like a sunny heaven.

Send lost objects
to the moon.
Instant pictures and parlor tricks.

The ache of twilight
dances
like wrestlers
on the barren earth.

Midday Marauders

Big bad love
is better than no love at all.
Stolen and fleeting.
Deliberate with consequence.

We don't think
in black and white.
Only in dark places,
under sheets
banging against each other,
swindled into lust.

Remember lighter days
when I wasn't
embezzling your face
and got more sleep.
Instead of filching
like bugs
we should've listened
to each thought
turn into noise
or maybe sounds that
we hadn't heard in a long time.

We hoped for a notion
to be ourselves
from the beginning
and stuck to the plan
like bank robbers.

Unplug the cameras.

I'll go to the vault.

Pray Let Me Know

Isabel, last month
we spent a dead end drinking our money away.
Laughing twin drinkers swapping stories.
Testing locals & bartenders with
trivia, fishing for pictures of Yeats,
leathercraft in the dust, glances for
empty beer glasses, full ashtrays,
growing stacks of postcards.
We left early enough to arouse suspicion
and jealousy from the moralistic crowd
came home still burning with questions,
checking books for more brilliance and invention.
Then, I wrapped my arms around your couch.
And in my head you appeared & spoke.
I twitched in my sleep looking for morning,
watery eyes dripped into my mouth.
At newest sight you were always work.
But, I am paralyzed now, awry in your apartment.
This poem grew from my ardour, our laughter,
Isabel. Also, to remind your current dictum
about the lure of the apple,
the Goddess of approaching drums
and drunken hubris.

The Pleasures and Pains of Lust

after Thomas De Quincey

It has been a long time since I first heard your voice,
your forgotten lips speaking of uncontrolled trysts,
the time before you decided to impersonate me,
made to forget all known dates, significant or otherwise.
But I knew you would remember, a head for numbers,
eyes for words told in stories, acted in afternoon drama,
always an unconscious minister of recited pleasure.
Those heart-quaking vibrations sewn into hands
like cigarette smoke broken lines, evaporated torments
reverting lowest depths, and ringing in my head.
I see a sad eyed jester in the midst of misery.
We practice at intermission and I jump out of bed
to splash cold water on my face. But cardinal
events are not to be forgotten, like you, celestial drug.

Lockstep Love

Covering ground again.

It's time.
Bedroom marching pleas.

Unison hum
like mosquito wings.

We want to be free legs.

Shadows from the city (repeat).

Stage play, moonlight dancer.
Grey barracks performance.

Think of something to say.
Then don't say it.

Inches on the body = miles on the mind.
Awaken on the firing range.

Tighten up
your twitching body.

Three Short Poems

Do You Love Me?

I have always thought piety
an unattractive quality.
And youth very heaven.

Bad Habits

Bad habits full blown
in old age compound
the things that I did
when youth stood around.

An Arrangement to Meet at a Rest Stop, Afternoon Rain

The skies were Irish today.
Our conversation was confused, silent, brief.
You wanted answers.
I wanted my things, my books, my clothes.
You forgot them, probably thought
you would never see me again.
You were right.

Months of Petals

March parades us with beauty
altogether well, slight breeze memory.

Crowds foresee our foibles
ground us in upper/lower worlds.

No choice but to drink mead
with stiff Ireland, sober no more.

This evil face. Underlined phrases
in books of Catholic literature.

Little trees, notes nailed to them.
Field writers with bowler hats, glances.

Given away myself a part of worlds.
Used like one thousand old and white stars.

Errors are petals of discovery, writes Joyce.

Milwaukee Afterparty I Should Have Avoided

And he was telling us about some personal lovethings,
how they had to get it all straight before he moved out here
from backeast dustcloud. Somewhere the rent didn't seem high
for a one room coldwater flat surrounded by the evilgrey
industrialcity with no rations for the sacred&religious.
Thinhipped bowing, sorted lookalikes walked around the room
trying plaidshirt notfitin, nervously searching for ways to make
breakfast out of breadloaf and eggwhites in the bluefridge.
Small apartments with cigarettes from red lipped openmouths.
Immense smokerings, thoughtbubbles, illuminated dumbtalk
from longbodies who hung over blackforest fire escapes
never realizing some lives had once (perhapstwice) passed by.
All the while he wrote desperate letters home to motherlovers
with shakenheads in disapproval. Reach for another bourbon.
And she went on again about her past, some jailkiddrug story,
all deafening rumors about best laid plans, reported accusations.
Words spoken so fast she was inventing new contractions. Then,
she called some guy a wannabe feminist. Shouts, blares, yammers
from outside convinced himself and others about the last nighthome.
Didn't sleep with her passedout on the couch. He could wake
her up with his eyes, his beerbreath, his fewdollars of weed
in the hollowedout sole of his shoe. Too sane for madmen,
not shallow enough for artschool, what his friends had become.
But they had nowhere else to go, all lovepromise and headsweat.
Taking wrongrisk, capable of doing horriblethings if needed.
And I was swimming, studying for midterms, standardizedtests,
the bias of thosethings. Therefore we left. And I said to Joan
as we rushed down the street to my safe blackcar. We were past
a ticktick in riotdream now. Droves of rivernoise in nightmaze.

The Land of Give and Take (Trinity)

You are my confessor, to whom I have entrusted my soul.
Dispel my illusions then by telling the truth; for truths of this
sort are very rarely told.

ST. TERESA OF ÁVILA, *The Book of Her Life*

…all a Lie; and I begin almost to think
there is no Truth or very little in the whole story.
JONATHAN SWIFT, *Journal to Stella*

Overture

"I went to the city to-day,
stopt at a bar to meet you and we staid there
with never any talk of treason, heartily."
Hapless sinners, unchecked passion
for fearful hearts, need for support system.
You're invited to a party,
drinks and billiards, supervision,
necessary classroom where the social and popular
talk of literature and minstrels,
a travelling band of wannabes in our own way.
Words and looks to make us more interesting,
a veiled happiness in trivia questions,
discussions, flirtatious parlor tricks
on advisable walks
just north of one of the widest parts of the river.
Let your mind be the widest part as well.
I've seen you around gathering information
from various classes, feigning interest
to noticeable quotes, saved decisions.
Lunch followed by pretending near library stacks.
What can you gain now?
Angels are servants of God
who have never tasted sin.
Hear the other side, see the other side.

Intermezzo

"I was adreamed, methought, that you were here
in search of the unvarnished truth."
Now I know why Cistercians take a vow of silence.
Study and prayer by mute monks.
Kneelers sans cushions, the path to enlightenment.
There are always confessors, soon called martyrs,
words whispered from lips behind closed doors.
Tell the hardest truth first,
the truth that clasps the earth.
Regression and impersonation.
Your desire to be envied and made mystery
like adults who drink import beers in bars,
take on other lives in order to survive.
Who knows what is best for us?
Friends who dictate (y)our decisions.
Shot up with sodium pentothal
to confess to the body, not the spirit.
"Discretion is necessary in everything.
I have seen nobody of consequence to know the truth."
I was so out of my head this morning
that I sent excuses about what I believe.
"Therefore pray, be kind.
Keep past stories in some safe place.
I would give something for their keeping."

Coda

"'Twas a terrible, windy day. We had
processions in carts of the Pope and the Devil,
and the butchers rang their cleavers.
It blows bloody cold and I have no waistcoat here.
Parliament prorogued, guiltless and still, and I tottered."
Does God give health for loves you lose?
Can silent dark sustenance ever sustain?

71

Thousands of martyred Jesuits scream around the world
with mood knowledge, central love status.
And what of your steamy letters?
I shall not answer them.
Replies might be fairly fuddled;
people began to prattle before I came away.
You said you received my letters. Don't tell me how many.
Instead, read the following like a diary entry,
an appearance or two in the *Selected Letters*,
or a narrative in circumstance.
We were too weak to support each other
trading fears for other fears.
We discover ourselves with great aims,
martyred in love's flaming heart.
"However, I must go as I came until it mends.
And so I walkt home as I went, and am got into bed:
I hope in God some rest will do me a little good."

III. The Exaggeration of Everything

But in all that what truth will there be?
Waiting for Godot, Act II

The Mystery and the Truth

For Edward R. Murrow

There was a man
who died on a road
near an old town
never to be remembered
for what he did
or who he knew
or how many friends he had
or which one of those friends
spoke at his funeral
which occurred
on a hot August day in 2008
outside of the city of M_____
at the Church of the Sacred Heart
following services
in St. Joan of Arc Cemetery
on quiet, little Lilac Street.
He will not be remembered
for his great deeds
or his sharp wit
or the thousands of dollars
he once donated to animal rescue
or the fact that he always
woke late
which angered his wife
who had been up
most nights nowadays
with a bad cough
watching the sun rise
and hoping that maybe today
would be the day
those damn creditors
would stop calling
now weeks

after the death of her husband
who had tremendous
debts all over town
mainly from gambling
and boozing, carousing
at local bars
with local ladies
who seemed to like
this man's company
an awful lot
and who most of the time
couldn't be trusted
to relay a story
like this accurately anyway.
So instead,
this man
will decay in some
grave in the Midwest
and never be feared
or followed.
He will never
say anything great
or do anything memorable.
He will never scale new heights
or reach new lows
because often we find
the truth to be so naked
that it screams to be clothed
in mystery.

Change the Gait of my Life

For Patrick Kavanagh

The horses gathered round the cold
pond and mingled on wide streets
where bars fill up with fake light.
When the settle bed was built for
my uncle, my aunt took comfort
in the fact that he wouldn't fall out
even when he came home from
the bar after walking from one end
of the neon soaked Mission street
to the other stopping in every bar
that didn't have a television blasting.
And sometimes he would even make
an exception to that rule. Each bar
was filled with road gossip and my
uncle would come home ready to
charge and argue with my grandpa.
And they would yell at each other
in that Irish way until one of them
was finally shut up by the other,
either by passing out or often by a
smack to the face, then to the ground
suddenly like the sun through
the morning fog. I always woke
to a next day that had these glances
at the breakfast table, these looks
like altar boys holding their tongues
in front of the priest. Thinking hard,
but speaking not. The smoke in the
light and dust in my eyes while my
uncle reached his dirty hands into
a glass of ice and placed a cube on
what my father called his cold steel
tongue. And then finally, after a long
silence came the great apology.
Something that my grandmother
demanded. Tainted waters might also
flow in the blood of the grand sun.

The Navigators

White stone Portugal,
the flight out to sea.
Belltowers and trade winds
filled by dreams to loot the soul,
a thousand saintly and pious eyes.
What is beyond Cape Bojador?
Perhaps monstrous men who fight
in the war for spice and cattle.
Ones who play cards and fish
on the coast of 100 miles
to win land for Iberia,
choke gold from the sand,
quarry marble for palaces,
mine rubies for Isabella's rosary.
And where is Aragon
on the newest map
approved by the Pope?
It is covered with rocks
and area treaties, sea routes
buried under oceans of water.
Someday stop by Madeira
and ask them why they are Catholic.
You might get a host of answers.

Long-sleeve Black Shirt

I had followers in that shirt
especially when I wore it many days
in a row, kept it safely on my
back as passers by pointed,
perhaps thought that
I was a transient or an artist.
Maybe a bearded Russian writer
who lived alone with only a plant,
a window and his pages.
A stone faced man
with no other clothes,
no hope for a Queen Clean Laundromat.
I have no change to plunk into any machine.
It was all given to the poor of heart,
the poor in spirit.
The ones who most ignore
and yet talk about in times of woe.
I am down to my last clean dish,
my last clean shirt,
my last clean thought.

Elizabeth Bowen's Rome

Italian walls
brittle that
walk in rose
cornelian.
Trees bloom
like a cistern
overflowing.
Factories make
shadows out of
dark clouds
and roads sing
like red tin ribbons
emptying sky
onto the ground.
I think I see
you Elizabeth
smoking a French
cigarette jotting
down descriptions
of truth from
the lips and eyes
of an angel.

More Swift to Run Than Birds to Fly

after James Elroy Flecker

I ignored the sun when
he told me to nix
my other life
on the threshold of morning
and went to see my body
awakened by blind
tears, the swarm of troubles
at year's end.
I heard a cough somewhere
in the distance.
It must be the boys
of Amber Street thriving
like pride in the alleys
of our minds,
smoking grey shadows
whispered into air.
The moon glow of summer
days reminds me
of trumpets calling
the feast of night,
red wine frozen like ghosts.
Let us dance like bodies
in the snow and sing
for the angels
of earth until our gardens
land near home
and sweet flowers decay
for new lips to speak,
new hands to feel.

The Development of History

Tell me, Rimbaud, about Abyssinia
about words and poetry
in the streets. Tell me about
the French mind where love and pain
are intertwined. Tell me
of history as told by poets who
drank and ate and fucked too much.
Tell the world who will not listen.
State with your eyes
the state of the nation, the tales
and problems of an age,
the beauty that was a fire sprung up
in fields littered with bodies
slow to dissolve among the living.
Tell me of a blackness broken
like the fingers of children
and trains through downtown.
Tell me of imagination, the politics
of persecution where death becomes
the only escape. Tell me now
before we grow beyond forty and hold
still with the innocent expression
of an irritable boy.

Thoughts in an Empty Bar
After Thanksgiving

Lost in time
on the continent,
a kick from the table leg,
moveable faces.

Be with me white angel.

This parable God,
with dead eyes.

Repertoire of empty
beer glasses
cracked.

All that runs,
runs well.

This long war,
land cleared,
darkling harbor,
blank sky woven into sleep.

I think of moonlight,
Beckett's tree,
Crane's bridge
and the exile of her streets.

High School Confessional

I read an article once
that was like an epistolary novel
where a young girl,
a member of the smokers
wrote to a dead boyfriend,
confessed her secrets,
and finally described the suicide
of her high school lover
who convinced her
to go all the way
in the dark moonlight
of a Nissan Sentra
after a summer party
had ended with the police
showing up and giving
out tickets to under-agers
corralled on the porch
in loose handcuffs.
The girl slipped her small hands
out of the metal rings
and they drove to a field,
felt each others
bodies in the back
of the silver car
while he thought of other girls
in skirts, or how
he couldn't tell his father
that he was out all night
instead of home
applying to colleges,
looking into wrestling
scholarships or packing
for the next match.

The next week
when she said,
"give me a ring sometime"
he just lost it and drove
to a secluded spot
with his father's only hand gun.
She went home
to write letters and saved
the handcuffs under her bed
in case she might need
them again, in case she wanted
to relive the strange
weather of that night,
the times she could only
remember in those letters,
those fictional letters.

Something I Heard

Once, a friend of mine told me
a story about his aunt.
How she often stayed glued to PBS,
but complained
about the length of programs
and her lack of chances to pour another drink
during a night of quality public television.
There was a pause
and then he said,
"Turns out she was an alcoholic.
After she died we found half full pill bottles
of scotch
in the medicine cabinet
under the bathroom sink
and in the closets."
Then there was a much longer pause.

The Sorrowful Mysteries

There are words that we save, whispers even, that stay in our minds
when all else has left us for dead in the middle of a winter storm
without a bottle of brandy to keep us warm until the minute before
we pass and leave a legacy that might be forgotten with hope that
it won't. But our friends try hard for the first few months, collect
pictures, stories of salutation and salvation, the agony in the garden,
the scourging at the pillar. Only days before my grandfather died
he looked at ease, or so I thought. He turned to me in the afternoon
light of his den when the television was on *mute* and said, "I don't
know if I should get better or just die." Then he looked to the door
to see if my grandmother was coming with his snack of carrot sticks,
water, and pills. We sat and listened to the silence for a while and
then he told me about his first car, the way it used to shake on the way
home late at night under a full moon. He always carried two cigars
on those trips out to his girlfriend's farm. One to give to her father,
one for the long trip home late at night after doing deliveries around
town in that shaky car. When I helped him to the bathroom he also
began to shake. He said it was from a mixture of panic and love.

Old Growth Forests like Days
in the Afternoon

I went to the bar early last night,
talked to a man about logging, about the wood industry.
He was missing three fingers,
kept scratching his chin with his knuckles
saying things like, "Well, the world sure has lost something,"
or "When pine was king we were his servants."
And it seemed to hurt this man
when he mentioned the cutting of trees,
the slowing of production, the itch in his hands
like he could still feel those fingers,
still see new light cut out of the earth.
After a few hours he bought me a shot and a beer,
thanked me for listening and walked to the door,
sawdust still on the back of his work shirt.
And I thought about life,
I thought about the tree of knowledge.
I thought about wood for homes,
wood for bookshelves,
wood for caskets.

Three Poems for Train Travel

Track One - Land

Streets and bridges desert grey.
Silos and dim red light crossings.
Men lay bricks from ladders in the sky
suspend over industrial rooftops,
dotted water pools like eyes.
Weeds grow over drain pipes
connect to dark cardboard houses.
Hills of gravel form frozen lakes.
The city, small distant buildings.
They look empty, dead trees,
wreckage from Midwestern lives.

Track Two - Car Jumpers

In winter white barns awaken with bramble
choking the sky. Chimney smoke,
distant fields of men in trench coats, empty boxcars.
One has a short cigar unlit.
He gnaws at it while the air duels itself.
Grain houses and fire barrels weep.

Track Three - Passengers

The man in a blue suit talks on his cell phone
and a conductor with bitter, strained eyes
pushes a cart with coffee and tea, water for kids
who look out the window to a prairie land moving
with infinite west. One asks, "Whose house is that?"
The mother replies, "A man who waits at the next stop."

Four Short Poems

It Began to Snow

It began to snow.
She dragged her finger
from the window pain
to finish putting lip gloss
on her lips,
then into her pocket,
slowly kissing
her reflection in the mirror.

Estate Sale

The glamour of attics,
sound of death.
Someone buys the story.
Dust smells like bourbon,
her drinking in secret.
Curtain cigar stench.
Diaries from 1944,
discharge paper soldiers
with alligator wishes.
Bid farewell to hutches,
sterling silver, beheaded dolls.
Mother has moved on.
Strangers sort accumulations.

Homage to the Lady with the Last Supper Tattoo

No empty
space
for a body
of work.
Travel
the world
on pirate ships,
bodies rest
and motion.
Crusaders
sold her skin,
a sadistic grin.
Apostles'
gaping holes.
Ticket box
two dollars.
Hammered on
sideshow wine.
In flesh,
make Jesus wink.
Salvation,
optional.

Marathon

Bumper stickers
announce new craze
in marathon running.
How many young joggers
know the origin of the word?

The Man Who Shot John Lennon

One of the first times I was in Ireland,
in Sligo, of all places,
I was in a pub near the Cathedral
and I was talking to some friendly Irish folk
among fellow English major travelers
from Omaha or some other typical Midwestern city
when someone started talking about John Lennon,
about his music and his life, his death
and I was trying to remember
who the guy was who shot John Lennon
and why said guy had bought a copy of *The Catcher in the Rye*
a few weeks before the day he stalked and gunned down
the ex-Beatle and musician outside The Dakota
and why couldn't I remember that guy's name.
But it was probably because I consumed far too many pints by this point
and it was late in the day and still as bright as ever
for I remember I could see the light coming through the windows
above the small red wood benches,
within the slight hint of cigarette smoke and conversation,
in front of the gentle, drunken smile I had on my face.
But then, I suddenly took a deep breath
and went off to the jax and when I returned, relieved,
I was clear headed and I remembered his name.
The man who shot John Lennon was Mark David Chapman
and he did it because he wanted to rescue the youth of the world
from the torture of Lennon's supposed adulthood,
the reality of a painful world,
the sudden realization that the older we get,
the less time we can spend in a bar,
and the less time we can devote
to discussions about poetry and music with friends,
the less time we have to drink away the days
while hoping for some truth to the Wilde desire
of never growing up completely.

And I was glad that I finally remembered his name.
So I immediately went to the bar and got another pint
to toast the Holden Caulfield's of the world
because at the time I was still in college
and didn't have to worry
about such trivial and useless things as growing old.

Postcard Written After Viewing the Book of Kells

Dear Janet–
Here I am in Ireland
enjoying the country,
but not the weather.
When we got back
to Dublin so late
I was afraid I wouldn't
be able to see this
old book. But the great
walled library is open
on Sundays during
the summer just
for tourists. Was I
ever glad. Coming back
soon from 8th C. Eire.
       Love, Louise

TYLER FARRELL was born in Illinois, grew up in Milwaukee, Wisconsin, was educated by the Jesuits at Marquette High School and Creighton University, and by layfolk at the University of Wisconsin-Milwaukee. He has published poems, essays, and reviews in many periodicals, and a biographical essay for James Liddy's *Selected Poems* (Arlen House, 2011). He teaches writing and literature at Marquette University and currently lives in Madison, Wisconsin with his wife Joan and their two sons. His first collection of poems *Tethered to the Earth* was published by Salmon Poetry in 2008.